A NOTE TO PARENTS ABOUT STEALING

Stealing is not merely unacceptable social behavior. In most cases, it is also illegal. Therefore, understanding the serious nature of this misbehavior is crucial to a child's survival and well-being.

The purpose of this book is to define what constitutes stealing. It is also to help children truly understand the negative impact of stealing on a thief as well as on a victim. Reading and discussing this book with your child can help him or her avoid stealing and all of the unwanted consequences it produces.

Stealing, in one form or another, usually begins at an early age. Believe it or not, this is good news. Usually the consequences of childhood stealing are not as serious as stealing in later years. Therefore, while suffering the consequences of stealing causes enough discomfort to modify future behavior, it is not completely devastating to a child's life.

Suffering the consequences of stealing is essential to eradicating the misbehavior. This includes making certain your child returns whatever he or she steals and then apologizes to the person from whom the item was taken. When it is impossible to return a stolen item, the item needs to be replaced.

This book belongs to:

ANDREW

Published by Scholastic Inc.
90 Old Sherman Turnpike, Danbury, CT 06816.

SCHOLASTIC and associated logos are trademarks and/or
registered trademarks of Scholastic Inc.

ISBN 0-7172-8585-5

First Scholastic Printing, October 2005

A Book About
Stealing

by Joy Berry

SCHOLASTIC INC.

New York   Toronto   London   Auckland   Sydney
Mexico City   New Delhi   Hong Kong   Buenos Aires

This book is about Karen and her friend Lennie.

Reading about Karen and Lennie can help you understand and deal with **stealing.**

Has anyone ever taken something that belonged to you and not returned it?

You are stealing when you take and keep
something that does not belong to you.

If someone steals from you:
- You might feel disappointed, frustrated, and angry.
- You might think that the person cannot be trusted.
- You might not want that person to be near your things.

It is important to treat other people the way you want to be treated.

If you do not want other people to steal from you, you must not steal from them.

Sometimes you might take something *by accident*.

You might borrow something and forget to return it.

You might take something without thinking about it.

The things you take accidentally need to be returned right away.

Sometimes people take things *on purpose.* They know what they are doing. They choose to steal.

Sometimes people steal *because they want something or because they think they need something.* They might think that they cannot be happy unless they have the thing they are stealing.

YOU STOLE THAT CANDY!
I WANT IT! BESIDES, I'M HUNGRY.
THAT'S NOT RIGHT!

Sometimes people steal *because their friends steal.*

They might think it is OK to steal because their friends do it.

They might not want to be different from their friends who steal.

They might think their friends will like them better if they steal.

Sometimes people steal *because they think what they do will not make a difference.* They think no one will notice. They tell themselves their stealing will not hurt anyone.

Sometimes people steal *because they are angry.* They want to get back at someone who has done something to hurt them.

Stealing is wrong. No matter why people do it, it is never OK to take something that does not belong to you.

Try to make things right if you have stolen anything. Return what you have stolen if it is not broken or ruined.

If it is broken or ruined, replace it or pay for it.

Tell the person you stole from that you are sorry. Then do not steal again.

It is important to treat other people the way you want to be treated.

If you do not want other people to steal from you, you must not steal from them.